Essential Life Science

CELLS

Richard and Louise Spilsbury

Heinemann
LIBRARY

Chicago, Illinois.

Edited by Nancy Dickmann and Abby Colich
Designed by Rich Parker
Original illustrations © Capstone Global
    Library Ltd 2014
Illustrated by HL Studio
Picture research by Tracy Cummins
Originated by Capstone Global Library Ltd
Printed in China by China Translation and
    Printing Services

17 16 15 14 13
10 9 8 7 6 5 4 3 2 1

Library of Congress Cataloging-in-Publication Data
Spilsbury, Richard, 1963-
  Cells / Richard and Louise Spilsbury.
      pages cm.—(Essential life science)
  Includes bibliographical references and index.
  ISBN 978-1-4329-7807-5 (hb)—ISBN 978-1-4329-7839-6 (pb) 1. Cells—Juvenile literature. 2. Cytology—Juvenile literature. I. Spilsbury, Louise. II. Title.

  QH582.5.S67 2014
  571.6—dc23   2012046447

Acknowledgments
We would like to thank the following for permission to reproduce photographs: Capstone Library: pp. 20 (Karon Dubke), 21 (Karon Dubke), 26 (Karon Dubke), 27 (Karon Dubke), 40 (Karon Dubke), 41 (Karon Dubke); Getty Images: pp. 12 (Nigel Pavitt), 17 (Cyril Ruoso/JH Editorial), 36 (Cosi Bella Photo), 38 (Thierry Dosogne); Photo Researchers, Inc.: pp. 4 (Dr. Tony Brain & David Parker / Science Source), 6 (Manfred Kage / Science Source), 7 (Roger Harris), 18 (Spencer Sutton / Science Source), 22 (hybrid medical animation / Science Source), 29 (Eye of Science / Science Source), 30 (Scott Camazine / Science Source); Shutterstock: pp. 11 (Guinet), 19 (Tony Campbell), 23 (Rido), 25 (beerkoff), 35 (Neveshkin Nikolay), 37 (Krzysztof Odziomek), 39 (Four Oaks), 42 (Maxim Petrichuk), 43 (Dave Pusey); Superstock: pp. 5 (© Minden Pictures), 8 (© Science Picture Co), 10 (© Ingram Publishing), 14 (© Science Photo Library), 15 (© Radius), 16 (© age fotostock), 28 (© age fotostock), 32 (© National Cancer Institute / Science Faction), 34 (© imagebroker.net).

Cover photograph of a fat cell reproduced with permission from Photo Researchers, Inc.: (SCIENCE PHOTO LIBRARY).

Every effort has been made to contact copyright holders of material reproduced in this book. Any omissions will be rectified in subsequent printings if notice is given to the publisher.

Disclaimer
All the Internet addresses (URLs) given in this book were valid at the time of going to press. However, due to the dynamic nature of the Internet, some addresses may have changed, or sites may have changed or ceased to exist since publication. While the author and publisher regret any inconvenience this may cause readers, no responsibility for any such changes can be accepted by either the author or the publisher.

Contents

What Are Cells? 4

What Are Microorganisms Like?. 6

Are All Cells the Same? 10

Cells for Protection. 14

What Is Inside a Cell?. 16

How Do Cells Work? 22

Why Do New Cells Form? 28

How Do Cells Work Together?. 36

From Cells to Organs 42

Glossary 44

Find Out More 46

Index. 48

Eureka moment!

Learn about important discoveries that have brought about further knowledge and understanding.

DID YOU KNOW?

Discover fascinating facts about cells.

WHAT'S NEXT?

Read about the latest research and advances in essential life science.

Some words are shown in bold, **like this**. You can find out what they mean by looking in the glossary.

What Are Cells?

Think of a house made from bricks. A brick is a part making up the whole, along with other bricks. Cells are a bit like the bricks or building blocks that make up your body and the bodies of all living things. But unlike bricks, cells are alive. They are the smallest units of living matter.

Each cell is a self-contained unit. It releases energy from food to power different life processes. These include growth and repair, **reproduction** or making copies of itself, getting rid of waste, and finding food.

These are single-celled organisms called **bacteria** on the tip of a pin. It would take tens of thousands of these cells to cover it.

Eureka moment!

In 1665 in England, Robert Hooke published a book of what he had seen through a microscope he had invented. In it he described the tiny pieces making up a thin piece of cork as "cells." This was because their square shape reminded him of the cells or rooms where monks lived in a monastery.

One or many cells

Most living things on Earth are made of just one cell, although many of them may live together in the same place. These are called **microorganisms**. The rest—anything from ants to the tallest trees—are made of many cells. They are **multicellular**. Having more cells allows an organism to grow larger and have a more complicated shape. This can help it survive in different environments.

DID YOU KNOW?

A human being is made up of around 100 trillion cells. That number is about 7,000 times the total number of people on Earth!

Whales are some of the biggest multicellular organisms on the planet.

What Are Microorganisms Like?

The smallest organisms on Earth are made of just one cell. They are called microorganisms because we can normally only see them through a microscope. There are different types of microorganisms. One type are **fungi**, which are related to the mushrooms we eat. Fungi include the yeast we use to help bread rise, and molds such as the ones in the air that turn old bread green! Other types of microorganisms include protists, bacteria, and **viruses**.

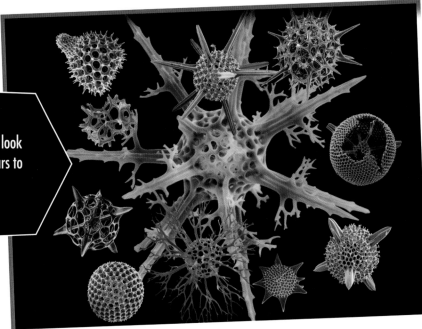

Diatom shells have shapes that look like anything from rods and stars to canoes and flying saucers!

Protists

Protists are a group of microorganisms that cannot be grouped with animals, plants, or other microorganisms. Some protists are like green plants because they make their own food using sunlight. These include **diatoms**, which live in oceans, lakes, and ponds. The outsides of diatom cells have interesting shapes and patterns of tiny holes in them.

Other protists are more like tiny animals because they hunt and move around. For example, **amoebas** wrap their body around even smaller microorganisms, trap them, and then eat them. Other protists can swim by moving tiny parts like hairs back and forth, almost like tiny oars!

DID YOU KNOW?

Not all single-celled organisms are tiny. Some discovered by scientists exploring the deepest parts of the world's oceans measure around 4 inches (10 cm). That's the size of an orange.

Eureka moment!

In 1683 in the Netherlands, Anton van Leeuwenhoek used a microscope to examine the plaque from between his teeth. He was amazed to discover different sorts of living things, which he called "animalcules." These were the first observations of bacteria.

Amoebas are shape shifters. For example, they can form arms to grip onto prey such as this bacterium and flatten into star shapes that float more easily.

Bacteria

Bacteria first lived on Earth around 3 billion years ago. Today, bacteria live everywhere on Earth, from frozen Antarctica to hot springs. Some bacteria are very useful, for example when they live on our skin and help keep away more harmful bacteria. Other types of bacteria help change milk into the yogurt and cheese we eat. But some bacteria can make people ill because they make chemicals that harm human cells. They cause anything from sore throats to more serious illnesses.

These streptococci bacteria cause sore throats and other serious diseases. They are ball-shaped and are found in groups held together as chains.

Viruses

Viruses are much smaller than bacteria. They are unusual microorganisms because they are not fully alive! They cannot feed, reproduce, move, or produce waste unless they are inside a living cell. Then they take over the functioning of the cell. When that cell reproduces, it makes copies of the virus too. Viruses cause many illnesses, such as flu.

Eureka moment!

In 1928, Alexander Fleming discovered penicillin, the world's first antibiotic (drug that can cure illnesses caused by bacteria). Before penicillin, people could die from even a small scratch or cut in their skin, because bacteria could get inside and infect the cells around the wound.

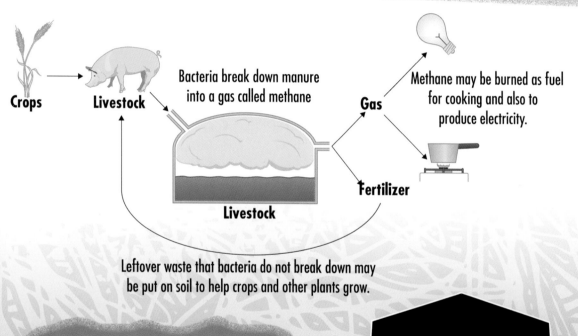

Crops **Livestock**

Bacteria break down manure into a gas called methane

Methane may be burned as fuel for cooking and also to produce electricity.

Gas

Fertilizer

Livestock

Leftover waste that bacteria do not break down may be put on soil to help crops and other plants grow.

DID YOU KNOW?

Adults have over 2 pounds (about 1 kg) of bacteria in their intestines. Most of these are very useful and help us to digest tough vegetables and other plant foods. This releases the nutrients we need to live and grow!

Some bacteria are very useful because they break down manure and other farm waste. They can make useful substances such as fuel and also stop waste from piling up!

Are All Cells the Same?

Multicellular organisms are made of many different types of cell, and each has different jobs to do. A cell's shape and structure is related to what it does.

For example, in animals, the major job of **red blood cells** is to carry **oxygen** from the lungs to cells all over the body where the oxygen is needed. A red blood cell's shape gives it a large **surface area** to carry oxygen. It also helps the cell slip smoothly through blood vessels while in the blood. On the other hand, plants need to take in water through their **roots** to survive. Root hair cells on plant roots have a long, thin shape. This gives them a large surface area for soaking up water from soil.

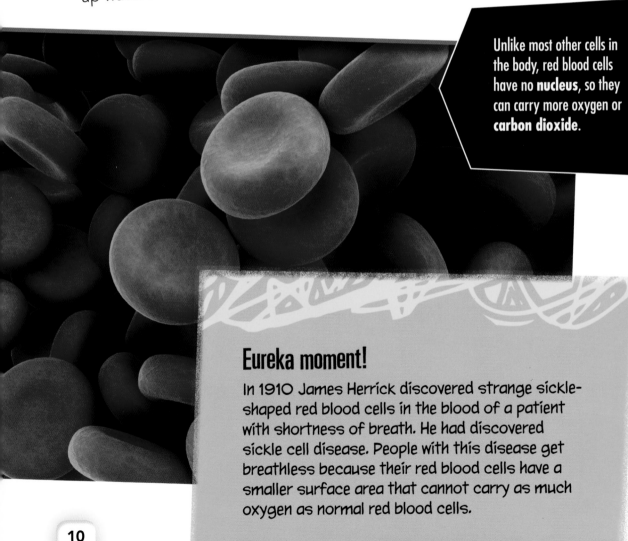

Unlike most other cells in the body, red blood cells have no **nucleus**, so they can carry more oxygen or **carbon dioxide**.

Eureka moment!

In 1910 James Herrick discovered strange sickle-shaped red blood cells in the blood of a patient with shortness of breath. He had discovered sickle cell disease. People with this disease get breathless because their red blood cells have a smaller surface area that cannot carry as much oxygen as normal red blood cells.

Cells for support

Some cells are specialized for supporting organisms. Bone cells make up the tough **skeleton** of many types of large animals. These cells produce and are surrounded by rings of hard **minerals** that give bones their strength. In trees the cells providing support are called fibers. These are long and tightly glued together to form wood.

Tall trees rely on the tough cells in wood to hold up their great weight and bend in strong winds.

DID YOU KNOW?

Scientists estimate that humans have about 210 different types of cells. Plants, including the tallest trees, only have around 140 types.

Cells for movement

Some cells look like they do because they are involved in movement. For example, muscles need to be strong to make body parts such as legs or wings move. This allows animals to walk, run, and fly to catch food or find safety. Muscle cells are stretchy so they can squeeze and release. They provide movement by changing their size and shape.

DID YOU KNOW?

The longest neurons in people run from their toes to near the brain, which is a distance of over 6 feet (1.5 meters) in tall people. Blue whale neurons could be 16 times as long!

Pythons rely on muscle cells to help them crush and then swallow their prey whole.

Cells for messages

Nerve cells, or **neurons**, are very long and thin. Their job is to carry electrical messages from different parts of the body to the brain, which is also made of neurons. Neurons all over the body are linked together to form a network of nerves. Neurons have branching ends that help them to hand over messages to each other very rapidly. This means that your brain can instruct your muscles to operate and work out what you feel, see, hear, smell, or taste in an instant.

Nerve cells pass on messages to other nerve cells, and muscle cells transform shape to provide strength and movement. Their different shapes are suited to their different functions.

Nerve cell

Relaxed muscle cell

Myelin sheath keeps messages from being lost, much like the plastic coating on a wire

Message passes from one neuron to another

Contracted muscle cell

Protein filaments pull in the cell, like rope tightening around a package

WHAT'S NEXT?

Scientists plan to treat injured people using stem cells. These are special cells that, once injected into injuries, can grow into different types of specialized cells, such as neurons. For example, this may mend damaged nerves in people with spinal injuries and allow them to walk again.

Cells for Protection

Some cells protect organisms by their shape. For example, skin cells are flat and overlap like tiles on a roof to form a waterproof layer over an animal's body. Other cells protect in different ways. **White blood cells** protect us from attack by microorganisms that enter through cuts or in the air we breathe. Some white blood cells hunt, catch, and eat bacteria. Others mark attackers with chemicals that make it easier for other cells to find and destroy them.

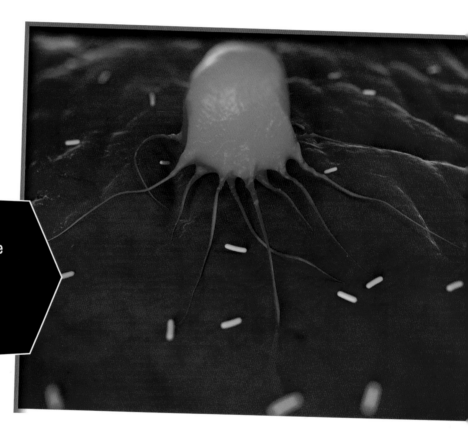

Look how similar the white blood cell is to an amoeba in the way it flows around and encloses its prey.

DID YOU KNOW?

Stinging nettle leaves are covered with sharp, brittle stinging cells containing toxin. When you brush against them, the tip pierces your skin and breaks off, and the toxin stings you.

Sting cells

Some organisms have special cells that sting other organisms. We keep away from jellyfish in the sea because their tentacles can sting us. Jellyfish sting to catch prey and to keep away animals that might want to harm them. Sting cells on the tentacles contain pouches of **toxins** (venomous chemicals) shaped like mini harpoons. The harpoon shoots out when an animal touches the cell. If it pierces the skin, the harpoon releases toxins into the animal!

WHAT'S NEXT?

Scientists have created a drug that kills harmful bacteria using chemicals found in an unusual jellyfish toxin. They hope to use the toxin to make medicines to treat heart disease too.

A large jellyfish like this can have millions of sting cells, but the most harmful jellyfish in the world is the size of a pencil sharpener. Its toxin is 100 times stronger than a cobra snake.

What Is Inside a Cell?

We have seen how different cells can be in their shapes and the jobs they do for multicellular animals. However, nearly all cells have the same basic structure.

The outer skin is called the **cell membrane**. It holds the cell together and passes water and chemicals in or out. The watery jelly inside the cell membrane is called **cytoplasm**. It contains many tiny bodies (called **organelles**) that carry out special jobs for the cell, in the same way that **organs** such as the heart and eye do jobs for our bodies. For example, **vacuoles** store water for the cell.

DID YOU KNOW?

Cytoplasm is around 80 percent water! It contains tiny filaments of chemicals that help retain the shape of the cell.

This is an animal cell. Can you see some of the parts making up a typical cell, including the cell membrane, cytoplasm, and nucleus?

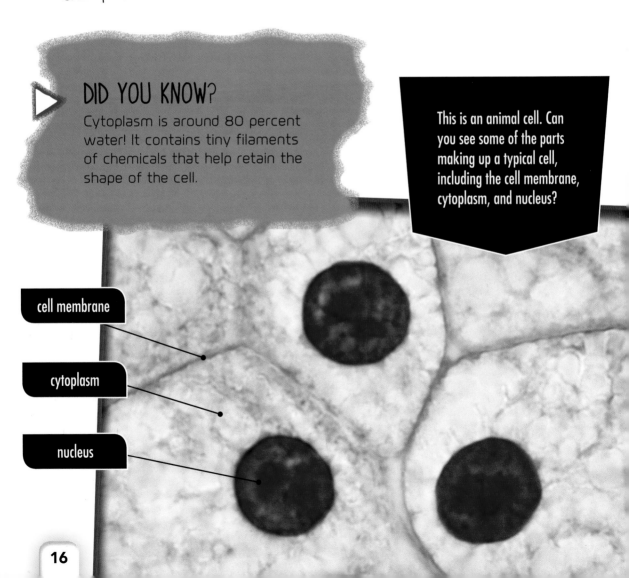

cell membrane

cytoplasm

nucleus

Controlling cell activities

All the activities that a cell carries out depend on strands of a special substance called **DNA**. DNA is made up of groups of chemicals arranged in patterns. These patterns together provide instructions about how a cell should build and maintain the organism it is part of. In most cells the DNA is bunched together into a body called the nucleus.

WHAT'S NEXT?

Scientists have bred goats that produce spider silk in their milk by adding spider DNA to the goat DNA! Spider silk is very strong and flexible and can be used to make bulletproof vests and repair human cells. Using goats produces much more silk than people could harvest from spiders.

DNA instructions in cells control how an organism such as this chimpanzee looks, how it grows, and how its body functions.

Plant cells

Plant cells have all the same parts as animal cells, but they also have some extra features. The first is that they have a cell wall surrounding the cell membrane. This wall is a tough box that is stiffened with very thin fibers. In the cytoplasm, a plant cell also has a large vacuole that may take up most of the space inside. The **cell wall** and vacuole work together to support the plant cell. The vacuole fills with water and presses outward to give the cell wall strength.

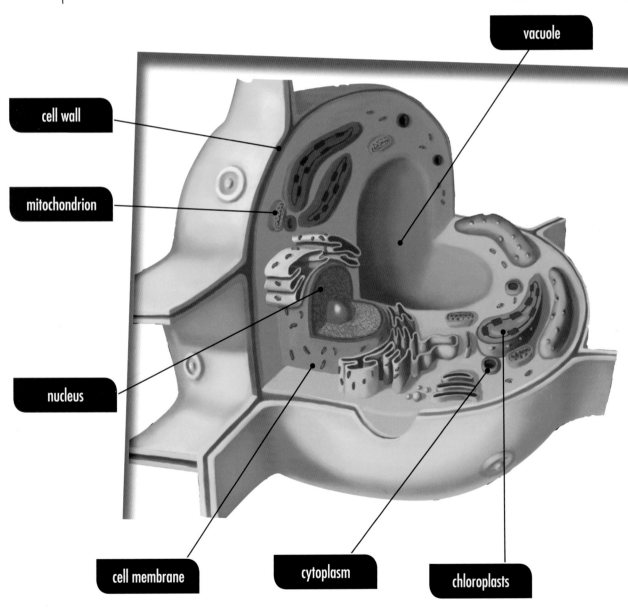

vacuole

cell wall

mitochondrion

nucleus

cell membrane

cytoplasm

chloroplasts

Food factories

Plant cells have up to around 100 small green organelles in their cytoplasm. These are called **chloroplasts**. Their job is to carry out a **chemical reaction** using water and carbon dioxide gas from the air. This reaction turns the ingredients into sugar that the plant can use as food. It can only happen if there is sunlight to provide energy for the reaction. The process is called **photosynthesis**.

Vacuoles can empty when a plant does not take in enough water through its roots. Then the plant can wilt because the cell walls are not supported.

DID YOU KNOW?

When making sugar through photosynthesis, plants also make oxygen. Most organisms on Earth need this gas to survive.

WHAT'S NEXT?

Scientists have found bacteria that can use photosynthesis to make oil using electricity as energy. In the future, people might be able to use these to make fuel for their vehicles when oil from the ground is running out.

Try This!

Follow these instructions to make a model plant cell. Making a model does not create an accurate cell because it is much bigger than the real thing and the parts may not be the right size and shape. But it can help you understand the structure.

What you need

- shoe box
- strong clear plastic bag just bigger than the box
- medium-sized balloon
- bicycle or other air pump with a long plastic pipe attached
- 2 strong elastic bands or cable ties
- 4 small paper clips
- 2 packets of jelly
- Heatproof jug with capacity of 3.5 pints (2 liters) or more
- long wooden spoon

What you do

(1) Place the jelly in the jug on a heatproof surface. Have an adult add hot or boiling water to the jelly and carefully stir to dissolve it.

2 Place the box on a hard surface. This will be the cell wall of your model cell. Put the plastic bag inside. This is the cell membrane. Use paper clips to fix the top edges to the sides of the box so the bag stays open and does not fall down.

3 Use a band or tie to attach the end of the pump tube firmly to the balloon. This needs to be waterproof. Place the balloon in the bag with the pump outside. The balloon is the cell's vacuole.

4 Carefully fill the bag with jelly to about two-thirds the height of the box. This is the cytoplasm. Close up the bag very firmly around the tube with a cable tie. Leave some empty space above the jelly. Leave the cell in a cool place for the jelly to set.

5 Slowly start to pump up the balloon vacuole. Check to make sure this does not force jelly out of the top of the bag, causing a mess! Does the box feel firmer? Can you imagine how a plant cell wall and vacuole work together to support a plant?

How Do Cells Work?

You have probably been told how important it is to eat breakfast so that you have the energy for a morning doing schoolwork or other important activities. All work uses up energy. To get energy, an animal eats food and a plant makes its own food through photosynthesis. But they can only access the energy in food with the help of tiny bodies called **mitochondria**.

Powerhouses

Mitochondria are dotted through all cells and are the powerhouses of living things. Inside the mitochondria a chemical reaction called **respiration** takes place. In respiration a sugar called **glucose** combines with oxygen to release energy as a type of chemical. Cells can use this chemical to carry out their functions. In people, the oxygen for respiration comes from the air that we breathe in. During respiration, carbon dioxide gas is produced. This can be poisonous if it builds up in cells, so we need to breathe it out.

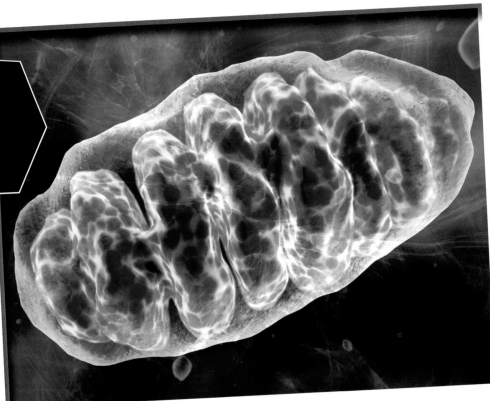

The respiration reaction happens on the many folds inside mitochondria.

DID YOU KNOW?

In sticky mud such as that found in estuaries, there is very little oxygen. So bacteria living there respire using other chemicals called sulphates instead of oxygen. Instead of producing carbon dioxide they produce hydrogen sulphide, which smells like rotten eggs!

Runners breathe heavily and fast in and out to take in oxygen so they get plenty of energy to run with. They also get hot because some of the energy made during respiration is released as heat.

In and out

At a bicycle factory, raw materials such as steel and rubber arrive and are used inside to make bikes. Finished bikes come out of the factory. People working in factories control how much raw materials are let in and how many bikes are let out. For example, if people do not buy many bikes in winter weather, then the factory does not need so many raw materials. Cells can also control what goes in and out, using the cell membrane.

sugar molecule

water molecule

membrane

membrane

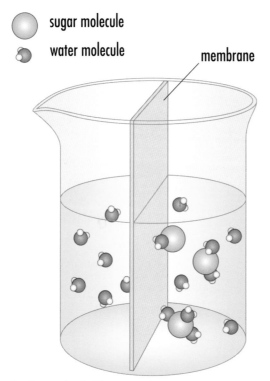

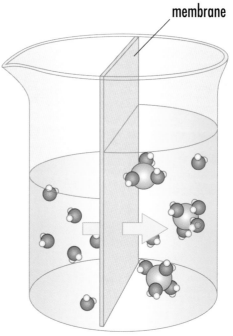

This beaker is divided by a membrane. On one side are water molecules, and on the other are water and sugar molecules in a solution. There are more free water molecules in the left-hand section.

Water molecules move from left to right to balance out the numbers in the two sections. The level is now higher on the right because more water has moved there.

This diagram shows how osmosis works. Water molecules move from where there are more free ones to where there are fewer to balance the numbers.

For example, water may move into the cell to fill a vacuole or to be used in chemical reactions in the cell. Water naturally moves from where there is lots of it to where there is less. It travels though tiny gaps or gates in the cell membrane in a process called **osmosis**. Other substances may move in different ways. For example, the glucose needed for respiration is carried into the cell by chemicals in the membrane.

Eureka moment!

In 1945, Willem Kolff built the first successful dialysis machine using parts he found such as tin cans and sausage skins. The dialysis machine is used by people whose kidneys do not work properly in removing harmful substances from their blood. The machine relies on osmosis to work.

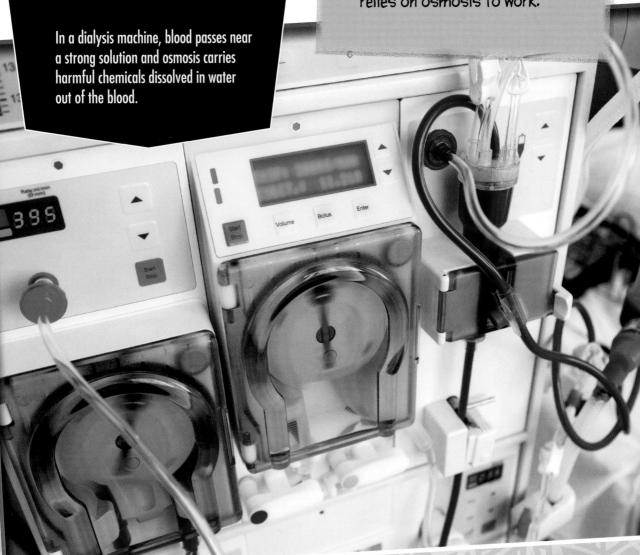

In a dialysis machine, blood passes near a strong solution and osmosis carries harmful chemicals dissolved in water out of the blood.

Try This!

It is tricky to see osmosis happening in one tiny cell. However, it is possible to demonstrate this important process using an egg with its outer shell removed! This reveals its cell membrane.

Prediction

Osmosis across an egg's membrane will allow water to move in or out.

What you need

- 2 uncooked chicken eggs
- 2 large glasses or jugs
- scales to weigh eggs
- 1 pint (0.5 liter) vinegar solution

What you do

1 Carefully place an egg in each glass or jug. Use the scales to weigh each egg plus jug. Record your data.

2 Pour the vinegar into one glass/jug and the same volume of water in the second.

3 Leave the glasses/jugs in a safe place for 48 hours. You should be able to see lots of small bubbles on the surface of the egg in vinegar. These are bubbles of carbon dioxide gas released during the chemical reaction between the vinegar and the egg shell. The reaction causes the shell to dissolve.

4 After 48 hours, carefully tip away the vinegar and water, keeping the eggs inside the jugs/glasses. Rinse off any bits of leftover shell from the egg that was in vinegar.

5 Repeat step 1.

Conclusion

You should find that the egg that was in vinegar is now heavier than at the start of the experiment.

The egg that was in vinegar got heavier because it had no shell and water moved across its membrane by osmosis. This is because there is a stronger solution inside the egg than in the vinegar solution. The egg that was in water did not change in weight because it still had its shell protecting the membrane.

Why Do New Cells Form?

We all need new cells! We need them to replace cells that get damaged, for example if we get injured, or cells that only last a short time. For example, stomach cells need to be replaced every two days. That is because the strong chemicals that break down food also damage the cells. The old stomach cells pass out in our feces, but old skin cells fall onto the ground. They make up most of household dust. Some old cells are not lost. For example, nail cells build up to help protect the sensitive tips of fingers and toes from bumps.

This starfish is regenerating five new arms on a single surviving arm.

Eureka moment!

In 1998, scientists discovered that human brains can grow new cells. Before this, many people believed that babies were born with around 100 billion brain cells that had to last them through their lives.

Cells to grow

The other main reason we need new cells is to grow. Living things grow fastest when they are young, for example growing longer bones and bigger muscles. They may also need new cells to grow new parts. For example, adult cows grow udders they can use to feed their young with milk.

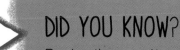

DID YOU KNOW?

Dust mites are tiny relatives of spiders that feed on dead skin cells in dust. An average mattress may have millions of dust mites inside, feeding on human dust! Every person sheds about 8 pounds (4 kg) of dead skin each year.

How new cells form

Most new cells form when living cells make copies of themselves. This process is called **mitosis**. The first stage in mitosis happens to the nucleus of the cell. Pieces of DNA in the nucleus make exact copies of themselves. Then the original DNA and the copied pieces move apart to opposite sides of the cell. The last stage is when the cell membrane starts to pinch the cell into two. In each cell the DNA forms a new nucleus.

DID YOU KNOW?

In the right conditions, some bacteria can reproduce as often as once every four minutes! But this is slow compared to some yeast cells. These can reproduce in less than a minute.

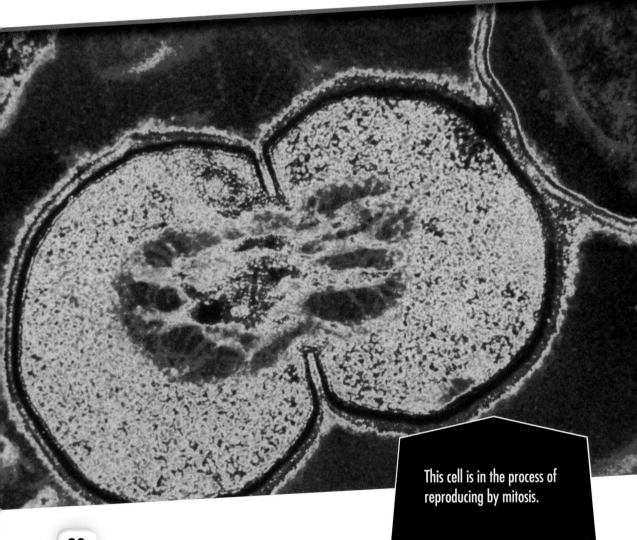

This cell is in the process of reproducing by mitosis.

New microorganisms

Microorganisms such as bacteria use mitosis to increase in number or reproduce. Each new bacterium formed by mitosis is a separate living thing that can move, feed, and carry out other important processes. Bacteria can reproduce very quickly in the right conditions, for example if there is plenty of food or in places that are damp and warm.

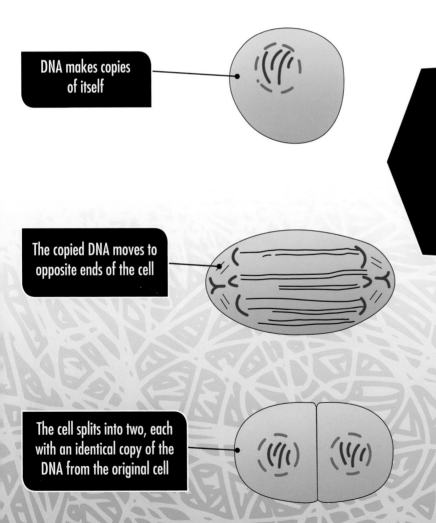

DNA makes copies of itself

Mitosis can be broken down into three stages. The first is making copies of DNA, the second is moving the copies to either end of the original cell, and the third is splitting into two cells.

The copied DNA moves to opposite ends of the cell

The cell splits into two, each with an identical copy of the DNA from the original cell

Dangerous cells

Cell growth is controlled by DNA. DNA contains instructions for when the cell should stop growing, start dividing, and die. But sometimes the DNA in cells gets damaged. This can happen accidentally during mitosis or because of something a person has done to affect their health, such as smoking cigarettes. Then the cells continue to grow larger than normal, divide out of control, and do not die when they are supposed to. These are **cancer cells**.

Cancer cells crowd out normal cells and clump together in groups called **tumors**. Tumors can grow into and damage the body's healthy **tissues**. Cancer can make people very ill. Doctors can treat some cancers by cutting out tumors and using medicines or other treatments to kill cancer cells. Then people's normal cells may start to repair their bodies.

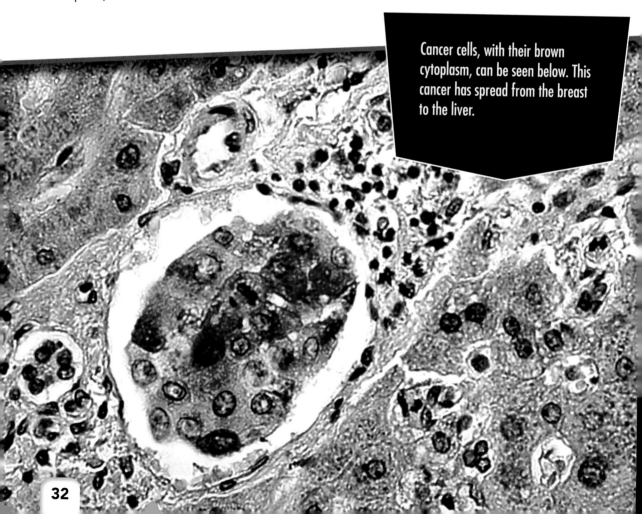

Cancer cells, with their brown cytoplasm, can be seen below. This cancer has spread from the breast to the liver.

WHAT'S NEXT?

Doctors have found a way for cancer drugs to attack just cancer cells. They inject the drug in tiny plastic particles. Cancer cells produce more chemicals called acids than normal cells. When a particle reaches a cancer cell, the acids break down the particle's outer layer, releasing the drug.

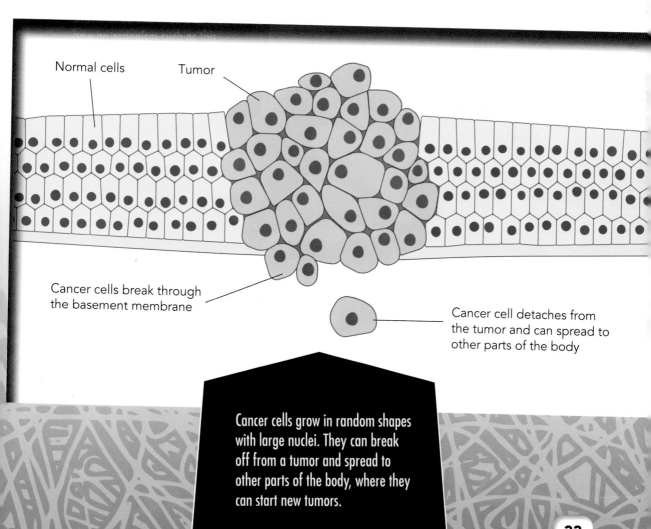

Normal cells

Tumor

Cancer cells break through the basement membrane

Cancer cell detaches from the tumor and can spread to other parts of the body

Cancer cells grow in random shapes with large nuclei. They can break off from a tumor and spread to other parts of the body, where they can start new tumors.

Sex cells

Many living things make special sex cells to reproduce with. Sex cells have half the DNA of most body cells. There are two types of sex cells, **sperm** and **eggs**. Adult males produce sperm, and females produce eggs by a process called meiosis. Sperm cells have a head containing a nucleus and a long, wiggly tail. Males produce millions of sperm. Eggs are large and round. They have a central nucleus surrounded by large amounts of cytoplasm.

In animals such as toads, the female lays eggs in water and the male then releases sperm to fertilize them.

Eureka moment!

In 2012 scientists discovered that women can grow more egg cells during their lives. Before that, people had thought that females are born with all the eggs they might need to have babies with during their lives.

Joining together

During sexual reproduction, sex cells join together. This is **fertilization**. One sperm fertilizes one egg. It burrows into the egg cell and its nucleus joins with that of the egg. The DNA from each sex cell combines. Now the fertilized egg has the same amount of DNA as other cells. It divides, and those cells divide again until they develop into a new living thing. It is different from either parent but has some things in common with each of them, such as eye color, as it has DNA from each.

DID YOU KNOW?

The yolk of an unfertilized ostrich egg is one of the largest single cells on Earth! It is the volume of about 25 chicken eggs. The egg white and the shell are not part of the cell.

A chicken egg, like the kind you find at the supermarket, is one large cell. A small, whitish disk on one side of the yolk contains the nucleus and most of the cytoplasm. The yolk is part of the cytoplasm.

How Do Cells Work Together?

People in a show have different roles, from the star performer to the person in charge of lighting or painting sets. They all work together for the success of the show. In the same way, cells in multicellular organisms have individual jobs to do but work together in groups called tissues.

There are many different types of tissue. For example, muscle tissue is made up of lots of muscle cells acting together and providing a stronger pull than a muscle cell on its own. **Epithelial tissue** is found all over our bodies, for example lining our mouths and forming our outer skin. It is made of a thin layer of tough cells tightly linked together. Epithelial tissues protect our bodies. If you ever go swimming in the sea, remember how useful your skin is at stopping water from soaking in and bacteria from sneaking into your body from the outside!

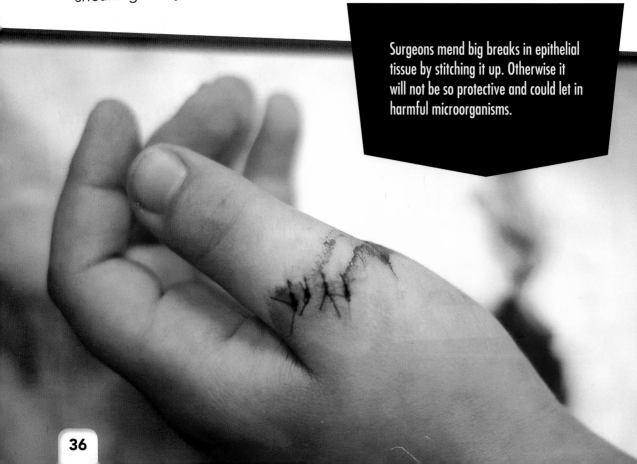

Surgeons mend big breaks in epithelial tissue by stitching it up. Otherwise it will not be so protective and could let in harmful microorganisms.

Fat tissue

Many animals, from whales to humans, have **adipose tissue**. This tissue helps to keep their insides at a steady, warm temperature when it is cold outside and cushions their insides from knocks and bumps. The fat in the tissue is also an emergency source of sugar for times when animals cannot get enough to eat.

DID YOU KNOW?

The thickest skin on your body is on the sole of your foot. It measures 0.1 inch (4 mm). This is very thin compared to a large whale shark that has skin up to 4 inches (10 cm) thick.

Whale sharks are the largest fish on Earth, measuring up to 43 feet (13 m) long. The tissue forming their giant skeletons is made from flexible cartilage—the same stuff that supports our ears and nose tips.

Tissues together

Some tissues work together for a single purpose for an organism. They form organs. For example, the heart is an organ just for pumping blood around the body to and from cells. To do this the heart has different layers of muscle tissue surrounded by a protective tissue bag filled with fluid. This stops the heart from bashing into other organs as it beats.

The eye is an organ specialized for seeing, and it contains many tissues. For example, muscle tissue in the colored iris makes it widen and narrow to control how much light gets into the eye. The retina is tissue that is sensitive to light that allows us to see.

The heart is a vital organ, which means a person dies if their heart stops working. These surgeons are repairing a heart that is no longer working properly.

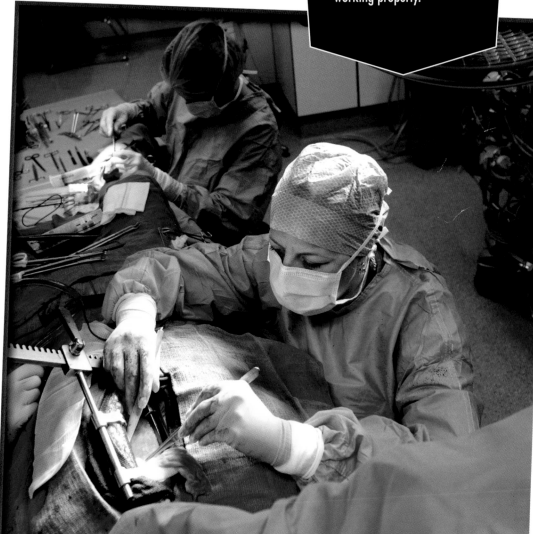

Organs together

Organs also work together with other organs to carry out different parts of complicated processes in organisms. They form organ systems. For example, the digestive system includes all the parts that taste and process food to release energy and nutrients that an organism needs. It includes the nose to smell, the tongue to taste and swallow, teeth to chew, and the stomach and intestine to digest food and get rid of waste.

Eureka moment!

In 1954, Dr. Joseph Murray and Dr. David Hume carried out the first successful human whole organ transplant in modern times. This means replacing an organ someone was born with using one from someone else. The doctors moved a kidney from one twin to his brother, whose kidneys were failing.

An elephant's trunk is its nose and upper lip. It contains around 100,000 different muscles, sensitive hairs, and cells. The trunk is strong enough to lift trees but sensitive enough to feel the softest touches.

Try This!

The leaves of plants are organs, and they are made up of different tissues. For example, the outer epidermis tissue is waxy to keep the leaf waterproof and has holes called stomata in it. These let carbon dioxide in for photosynthesis and control how much water vapor (gas) the leaf has inside. But where are the stomata located?

Prediction

Stomata are on the bottom of the leaf because if they were on the top, then water could more easily escape in the sun's rays that shine from above.

What you need

- 2 identical narrow baby food jars
- marker pen
- vegetable oil
- ruler
- petroleum jelly (Vaseline)

- 2 similarly-sized cuttings from a geranium or basil plant with about 4 large leaves with a stalk of at least 2 inches (5 cm)
- vegetable oil
- teaspoon

What you do

① Fill up each jar with tap water to about 1 inch (2.5 cm) from the bottom. Stand them on a level surface and mark the level carefully with the marker pen.

② Take one cutting and use your finger to smear a thin layer of Vaseline only onto the top surface of each leaf. With the second cutting smear the Vaseline only onto the bottom surface of each leaf. REMEMBER: Vaseline contains oil and can leave marks on clothes and other surfaces.

3 Place one cutting in each jar and put a teaspoon of oil into the water. This forms a layer that stops the water from evaporating, or turning to gas, during the experiment.

4 Place the jars with leaves into a light place away from direct sun and check the water level every 24 hours. If the water level has dropped, measure the distance below the water level at the start of the experiment marked on each jar. Record your results.

Conclusion

You should find that the water level around the plant with Vaseline on the bottom of its leaves stays the same. This is because Vaseline blocks the stomata so that the plant cannot take in carbon dioxide and get rid of water. Then they do not suck up water through their stems so fast. On the other plant Vaseline is not blocking stomata, so it sucks up water from its jar.

From Cells to Organs

A bike does not work very well if the chain is rusty or the tires are flat. It is unsafe to ride if the brakes are broken or if it has no lights at night. All parts of an organism are interconnected, similar to the parts of a bike. When one part goes wrong, it can affect the whole organism. This begins with cells. Tissues can only carry out their jobs if the cells they are made from work, and organs rely on healthy tissues.

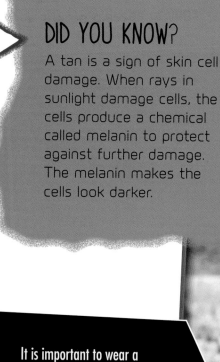

DID YOU KNOW?

A tan is a sign of skin cell damage. When rays in sunlight damage cells, the cells produce a chemical called melanin to protect against further damage. The melanin makes the cells look darker.

It is important to wear a helmet when cycling to protect your delicate brain tissue if you fall off and bash your head.

Caring for your cells

You can take care of your cells to make sure that your body remains healthy and your tissues, organs, and organ systems are working as well as they can. Drinking plenty of water helps make sure there is enough for cells to carry out osmosis and other important processes. Eating a healthy, balanced diet supplies the glucose and nutrients cells need to respire, grow, and reproduce. Avoiding too many sugary or fatty foods helps to stop our bodies from making too much adipose tissue. Keeping covered up in the sun and wearing hats and sunblock protects skin cells from being damaged by sunlight, and it can stop normal cells from changing into cancer cells.

The survival of these lion cubs depends partly on learning about dangers in their environment, but also on getting enough nutrients and exercise for their cells, tissues, and organs to function properly.

Glossary

adipose tissue type of connective tissue that contains stored fat

amoeba type of microorganism that captures food by flowing around it

bacteria microscopic single-celled organism. Some bacteria are useful, but others cause illnesses.

cancer cell abnormal cell that grows faster and bigger than normal cells, which the cancer kills

carbon dioxide type of gas found in air that is produced by living things during respiration

cell membrane thin layer similar to a skin around a cell

cell wall stiff layer on the outside of plant cells

chemical reaction when two or more substances combine to form different substances

chloroplast tiny structure found in green plant cells where photosynthesis happens

cytoplasm jelly-like material in a cell enclosed in the cell membrane

diatom microscopic protist that lives in water and can produce food using sunlight, similar to plants

DNA chemical in cells that contains instructions on how a cell functions and what an organism is like

egg female sex cell in animals

epithelial tissue tissue that covers the whole surface of the body

fertilization when DNA from one parent combines with that from another so that a new organism can develop

fungi type of organism similar to a plant but with no leaves, chloroplasts, or flowers that usually grows on waste or plants

glucose simple kind of sugar that plants can make and animals get from food and that is essential for respiration

microorganism tiny living thing that is usually made of one cell

mineral substance found in soil that is not produced by living things but which is important for their healthy growth and development

mitochondria tiny bodies in cells that release energy from food through respiration

mitosis process in which cells make exact copies of themselves. This is vital for growth and repair.

multicellular made of many cells

neuron long, thin cell found in nerves and the brain that passes along messages

nucleus tiny body in most cells that controls how they work

organ part of the body such as the heart made from several tissues that together carry out a particular job

organelle specialized part of a cell, similar to an organ

osmosis when water moves through a membrane because there are different amounts of dissolved substances on either side of the membrane

oxygen type of gas found in air and made by green plants that is essential for respiration

photosynthesis process by which green plants make glucose and oxygen from carbon dioxide and water using energy from sunlight

red blood cell type of cell in blood that transports oxygen and carbon dioxide through the circulatory system

reproduction ability to produce offspring or young

respiration process in living things that releases energy from food

root structure that can hold plants in soil and take in minerals

skeleton set of bones that support, protect, and allow movement in some types of animals

sperm male sex cell in animals

surface area total area of the surface of an object

tissue group of cells of the same sort, such as muscle cells, that do a job together

toxin type of substance harmful to cells and processes in living things; sometimes called poison

tumor abnormal growth of tissue resulting from uncontrolled multiplication of cells that do not help the body to function

vacuole small space in a cell that can fill with water

virus tiny microorganism that is not fully alive and which causes illnesses such as colds and diseases

white blood cell special type of cell in blood that helps organisms get rid of germs that cause illnesses

Find Out More

Books

Keyser, Amber J. *The Basics of Cell Life with Max Axiom, Super Scientist.* Mankato, Minn.: Capstone, 2009.

Latham, Donna. *Cells, Tissues, and Organs.* Chicago: Raintree, 2008.

McManus, Lori. *Cell Systems.* Chicago: Heinemann Library, 2011.

Sohn, Emily. *A Journey Through the Digestive System with Max Axiom, Super Scientist.* Mankato, Minn.: Capstone, 2009.

Somervill, Barbara. *Animal Cells and Life Processes.* Chicago: Heinemann Library, 2011.

Web sites

www.californiasciencecenter.org/FunLab/FunLab.php

At this web site of the California Science Center in Los Angeles, you can find links to interactive games to do with cells and science, and you can find some do-it-yourself science ideas.

www.centreofthecell.org/interactives/cellturnover/index.php

This web site is a game that gives you an idea of how fast different types of cells carry out mitosis.

www.centreofthecell.org/interactives/exploreacell/index.php

This site has a game that helps you explore the different tiny bodies within cells and the tasks they carry out.

learn.genetics.utah.edu/content/begin/cells/scale/

Have you ever wondered how big cells actually are compared with other things? Then visit this web site and move the slider.

www.smm.org/tissues/

This web site helps you learn more about tissues.

Places to visit

There are many great science museums around the United States—maybe there's one near you!

You can learn about cells and life, as well as other aspects of science, at the Museum of Science and Industry in Chicago. Many exhibits are interactive, so you can participate in the science yourself!

The Museum of Life and Science in Durham, North Carolina, has more than 75 animal species. Hands-on activities take visitors through the process of using scientific tools and conducting scientific inquiry. And you can watch real scientists as they conduct their research!

At the hands-on "Cell Lab" gallery at the Science Museum of Minnesota, you can put on a white coat and goggles and carry out science experiments all about cells!

Further research

You can find out lots more information about cells and the jobs they do. Try researching some of the following areas, using the web sites and books on the opposite page to help you.

Explore in more detail how neurons work and the structure of the brain and spinal cord. Then find out the impact of dementia and back injuries on the functioning of nerve cells.

Find out how twins and identical twins can be produced by sexual reproduction.

Research the following organs and tissues to see how they work and what their special features are that help them do a job for your body: liver, cornea, kidney, teeth.

Discover more about stem cells and how they may be used to improve health in the future.

Index

adipose tissue 37, 43
amoebas 6, 7

bacteria 4, 6, 7, 8, 9, 14, 15, 19, 23, 30, 31, 36
bone cells 11
brain 12, 13
brain cells 28
brain tissue 42

cancer cells 32–33, 43
carbon dioxide 19, 22, 40, 41
caring for your cells 43
cartilage 37
cell membrane 16, 18, 24, 25, 30
cell structure 16
chemical reactions 19, 22
chloroplasts 18, 19
cytoplasm 16, 18, 19, 32, 34, 35

damaged cells 28, 32, 42, 43
dialysis machines 25
diatoms 6
digestive system 9, 39
diseases and illnesses 8, 9, 10, 32–33
DNA 17, 30, 31, 32, 34, 35
dust mites 29

egg cells 34, 35
elephants 39
energy 4, 19, 22, 23
epithelial tissue 36
experiments 20–21, 26–27, 40–41
eyes 38

fertilization 35
fibers 11, 18
Fleming, Alexander 9
fungi 6

glucose 22, 25, 43
growth 29, 32

heart 38
Hooke, Robert 4
humans 5, 9, 11, 12, 13, 28, 29, 34, 36, 37, 38, 39

jellyfish 15

Leeuwenhoek, Anton van 7

meiosis 34
melanin 42
microorganisms 4, 5, 6–9, 14, 31, 36, see also bacteria; viruses
mitochondria 18, 22
mitosis 30–31, 32
multicellular organisms 5, 10–15
muscle cells 12
muscle tissue 36, 38

nail cells 28
nettles 14
neurons (nerve cells) 12, 13
new cells 28–31
nucleus 16, 17, 18, 30, 33, 34, 35

organ systems 39
organ transplants 39
organelles 16, 19
organs 38–39, 40, 42
osmosis 24, 25, 26–27, 43
oxygen 10, 19, 22, 23

penicillin 9
photosynthesis 19, 22, 40
plant cells 18–21
protists 6
pythons 12

red blood cells 10
respiration 22, 23, 25
root hair cells 10

scientific research and advances 13, 15, 17, 19, 31, 33
sex cells 34–35
sickle cell disease 10
single-celled organisms see microorganisms
skin 36, 37
skin cells 14, 28, 29, 42, 43
specialized cells 10–15
sperm cells 34, 35
starfish 28
stem cells 13
sting cells 14, 15
stomach cells 28, 33
stomata 40, 41
sulphates 23

tissues 32, 36–38, 40, 42, 43
toxins 14, 15
trees 11
tumors 32, 33

vacuoles 16, 18, 19, 25
viruses 6, 9

whale sharks 37
whales 5, 12
white blood cells 14

yeast 6, 30